Bigfoot Survival Guide

WILLIAM JEVNING

DEDICATION

To all who seek adventure and knowledge.

CONTENTS

ACKNOWLEDGMENTS

My thanks to the following people: Justin Mark, Jerry Bishop, Ruth Ackland, Todd Rawlins, Dan Ronald, Eric Hibbs, Jason Roberts, Jay Raymond, Adam Lima, Tom Dunsmoor, Doug Cochran, Ragnar Cochran

1: WHY A BIGFOOT SURVIVAL GUIDE?

The person who just opened this book to see what this is all about, must be asking why in the world do I need a "survival guide" for something that surely does not even exist?

That is a very good question, and you are a step ahead of those who would not even consider this question. My intention in writing this book is the safety and well-being of all persons venturing into forested regions. The question of the existence of what we commonly refer to as "Bigfoot" is not nearly as important as the question of why take a chance of possibly endangering myself or my loved ones should I actually encounter something that is "not supposed to exist"?

In the following pages, I will provide some background about the creatures, then methods of preventing any negative outcomes of encounters.

Most fictional creations have very shallow historical foundations, being at most a few stories. Bigfoot however has an extensive historical record not only in North America, but around the world.

Possibly one of the earliest references comes from the Bible, in the book of Genesis. In Ivan Sanderson's 1961 book Abominable Snowmen Legend Come to Life published in 1961, chapter 17 discusses this. Sanderson had a good friend that was a Jewish rabbi and scholar he asked about the creatures in ancient texts. This scholar, Rabbi Yohan N. ibn Ahron, said from the Bible and commentaries the following:

Many today believe in the Bible the name Nephilim refers to the giant Wildmen we think of as Bigfoot; however this is defined by the Rabbi. First he states that "Nephilim" is often translates as giants, but the commentaries state that this is not a name but rather an action, he says: "Nephilim is often translated as "giants" but the commentators tell us that they were called so because men would fall (nophel) on their faces with fright at the sight of them. Now here is the distinction, he goes on to say: The Giborim, who are later on referred to as Giborim Tsayid, are reputed to have been as tall as a tree", clearly not a Bigfoot, but he continues: In contrast there were creatures that plagued the Israelites during Exodus, they were the Sheidim – the Destroyers – who had been known to the patriarchs (Abraham, Isaac and Jacob) as the Seirim – the Hairy ones.

In America there are 574 recognized Native American tribes, nearly all of them have names for the Wildmen of North America. Here is a partial list of names:

Windago – The hairy man

Nant'ina

Get'quin

Nantiinaq

Urayyuh

Gilyuk

Kushtaka

Matlose

Goo teekli

A hoola hul

Gogit

Snanaik Boqs

Bukwas

Dzonoqua

Tsonoqua

Slalakums

Sokqueatl

Soss-q-atl

Neginla eh

Tornit

Sne nah

Bushmen

Lariyn

Tsadjatko (Giants, Skukum strong, powerful, dangerous being)

Hecaitomixw (Devil of the forest)

Stick Indians

Sasahevas

Hoquiam

S'oq'wiam (Wildman of the woods)

See'atco/Kauget (one who runs and hides)

Te Smai'Etl Soqwaia'm

Sami Soq'wai'm

Miitiipi (An undesirable sight which portends bad luck or disaster)

El-Ish-Kas

Tsiatkp

Stet'l

Tah-tah-kle-ah (Owl woman monster)

Ste ye mah, Seat ka

Yidyi'tay (Wildman)

Xi'lgo (wild woman)

See-oh-mah

Neglina eh (wood man)

Madukarahat (Giant)

Loo poo oi'yes'

Oh-mah

Tso apittse'

Nun Yuni Wi (the stone man)

Kecleh-kudleh

Ge no sqwa (the stone giants)

Windego (wicked cannibal giant)

Rigaru

Chy tanka

Chiha tanka

Kashehotapalo

Nalusa Falaya

Wetiko

Nu'numic

Tse' nahaha

Gougou

Iktomi

Esti Capcaki

Ye'iitsoh

So'yoko

Manabai'wok

Koktshe, Witiko, Atshen

Mesingw

Misinghalikun

Wsinkoalican

Toyona

The list goes on, but for this writing the names listed above provide the reader with some idea of the historical context of the creatures we are concerned with here. Native tribes from Alaska to the east coast of the United States have names for the creatures, and regard them highly within their cultures.

Europeans learned about them when they began traveling to the American continent, In a boot titled Noticias De Nutka, Jose' Mariano

Mozino was an official botanist/naturalist on an expedition of Juan Francisco de la Bodega y Quadra who was sent to investigate the Spanish limits of the North of California in 1792. He encountered natives at the Nootka Sound near Vancouver Island; here is a passage from this book:

"I do not know what to say about Matlox, inhabitant of the mountainous district, of whom all have an unbelievable terror. They imagine his body as very monstrous, all covered with stiff black bristles; a head similar to a human one, but with much greater, sharper, and stronger fangs than those of the bear; extremely long arms; and the toes and fingers armed with long curved claws. His shouts alone (they say) force those who hear them to the ground, and any unfortunate body he slaps is broken into a thousand pieces."

There is another reference in a book by David Thompson, titled David Thompson's Narrative of his Explorations in Western America 1784 – 1812.

"1811 January 5th. Thermometer – 26 very cold. Having secured the goods and provisions we could not take with us, by 11 AM set off with eight sleds, to each dogs, with goods and provisions to cross the Mountains, and three horses to assist us as far as the depth of the snow will permit. We are now entering the defiles of the Rocky Mountains by the Athabasca River, the woods are of pine are stunted, full of branches to the ground, and the Aspin Willow not much better: Strange to say, here is a strong belief that the haunt of the Mammoth, is about this defile, I questioned several (native peoples), none could positively say, they had seen him, but their belief I found firm and not to be shaken. I remarked to them, which such an enormous heavy animal must leave indelible marks of his feet, and his feeding. This they all acknowledged, and they had never seen any marks of him, and therefore could show me none. All I could say did not shake their belief in his existence.

On January 6th. We came to the last grass for the horses in Marshes and along small ponds, where a herd of Bisons had lately been feeding; and here we left the horses poor and tired, and notwithstanding the bitter cold, they lived through the winter, yet they have only a clothing of close hair, short without any fur.

January 7th. Continuing our journey in the afternoon we came on the track of a large animal, the snow about six inches deep on the ice; I measured it; four large toes of four inches in length to each a short claw; the ball of the foot sunk three inches lower than the toes, the hinder part the foot did not mark well, the length fourteen inches, by eight inches in breadth, walking from north to south, and having passed about six hours. We were in no humor to follow him: The men and Indians would have it to be a young Mammoth and I held it to be the track of a large old grizzly bear; yet the shortness of the nails, the ball of the foot, and its great size was not that of a bear, otherwise that of a very large old bear, his claws worn away; this the Indians would not allow. Saw several tracks of Moose and Deer."

Thompson does not mention the front feet of the animal, which is a dead giveaway if it was in fact a bear. We should also note that bears are hibernating that time of year, and the Indians would certainly know the tracks of a bear.

One more historical writing is from a book titles Wanderings of an artist among the Indians of North America by Paul Kane, published in 1847.

" When we arrived at the mouth of the Kattlepoutal River (today the Lewis River), twenty six miles from Fort Vancouver, I stopped to to make a sketch of the volcano, Mt. St. Helens, distant, I suppose about thirty or forty miles. This mountain has never been visited by either whites or Indians; the latter assert it is inhabited by a race of beings of a different species, who are cannibals, and whom they hold in great dread; they also there is a lake at its base with a very extraordinary kind of fish in it, with a head more resembling that of a bear than any other animal. These superstitions are taken from the statement of a man who, they say, went to the mountain with another, who was eaten by the 'Skoocooms,' ot evil genii."

In my book Notes From the Field I chronicled articles all throughout the time frame starting at 1811 to the 1950's from each decade, so there has been a consistent record from ancient times to the modern era of these creatures.

So the next question is, is there any proof of the existence of giant primates? The answer is yes. In 1935 G.H.R. von Koenigswald discovered 35 fossil teeth in a Chinese market. He published his findings in a publication titled Gigantopithecus Blacki, volume 43 part 4 Anthropological papers of the American Museum of Natural History New York, 1952. His scientific paper discusses his findings, and the species now known as Gigantopithecus Blacki is a recognized species. The Gigantopithecus while not Bigfoot, certainly establishes that not only have there been giant species of primates in east China, but it was much larger than what thousands of eye witnesses tell the sizes of creatures they saw, so The existence of a large primate in North America is not out of the question. Science is far from knowing even how many species of primates have existed.

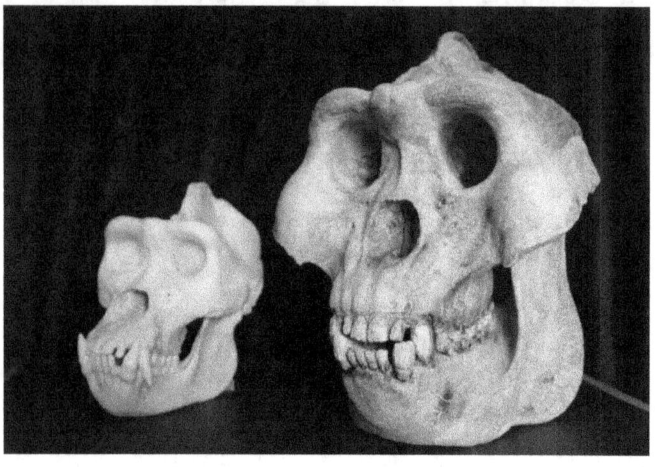

Left is a Gorilla skull, right is the skull of a Gigantopithecus.

2: What is Bigfoot?

Basic profile:

Size: Adults range between 6 feet and 10 feet in height.

Weight: Weight has been something guessed

at by witnesses, but may be very inaccurate based on observation alone. Many witnesses have estimated the weight of the creature (s) they saw between 300 to 1000 pounds.

A good example of weight calculations being inaccurate is with the Patterson Sasquatch mentioned previously. Many who have postulated this question usually guess the creature weighed approximately 300 pounds. However Patterson walked a 1300 pound horse next to the creature's fresh footprints, the horse did not make as deep foot impressions as those of the Sasquatch; this indicated the Bigfoot was heavier than the horse.

Humans are the exception in the primate world in regard to muscle and bone density, other large primate species have much higher densities and are heavier than they appear. It is likely a Sasquatch could weigh upwards of 2500 pounds.

Color: Bigfoot has been reported as being Brown, reddish brown, black, gray and white. Of calculations by reports 70 percent are reported as a reddish brown or cinnamon color. Juveniles most often are jet black.

Hair: Hair lengths have been reported as being different lengths on various parts of the body. Sometimes long hair is reported hanging from the arms. One variation is even bald on top of the head.

Facial features: Often the Sasquatch is describes as apelike in appearance, having a flat face, dark animal like eyes, a flat nose and no lips as in humans.

Distribution: The Sasquatch or Bigfoot has been reported all across North America and in every part of the world, the exception being Hawaii and Antarctica.

So just what is Bigfoot? Unfortunately since it's not yet a recognized species, there are as many opinions as there are people to offer one. We should remember that the Gorilla was not a recognized species until the beginning of the twentieth century, and similar stories circulated about gorillas in similar fashion to Bigfoot.

Let's start with n a general description. I mentioned that science does not know just how many species of primates have existed in the past, so is Bigfoot a primate?

Primates, like most species are classified by physical characteristics. Bigfoot shares the same physical characteristics as humans, apes and monkeys, and once recognized by science will be placed into the classification of primates.

To provide a physical description let's start with the best photograph to date of one, this is a still photograph from a film shot by Roger Patterson on October 20, 1967 at Bluff Creek California. It shows a female Sasquatch.

While sharing many of the same physical characteristics as both humans and other non-human primates, Bigfoot is something different. Like other non-human primates its forearms are longer than those in humans, also its upper legs are longer with shorter lower lags. They also have a long torso, head that may or may not exhibit a point or sagittal crest like Gorillas have. The Sagittal crest is prominent because it is the anchor for large jaw muscles. The Sasquatch hip bones are different than those of humans; we know this from their gait. Humans walk with our toes pointed outward, while the Sasquatch walk in nearly straight lines.

For humans this way of placing our feet

during walking is nearly impossible and demonstrates a different bone structure.

It is often claimed when someone finds Bigfoot footprints, that it's nothing more than bear tracks. Claimants overlook one very important factor in bear tracks, and that's the presence of the bears front feet, and that in lines of bear tracks each consecutive impression is very close to the next, the following photographs are an example.

(Black bear front and rear footprints)

(Black bear footprints)

Bear tracks usually show claw marks as well while Bigfoot tracks do not. Another claim is that overlapping bear tracks are what make what people claim are Bigfoot footprints. I looked at many lines of bear tracks, and if those finding such impressions totally ignore the obvious front and rear bear tracks I previously mentioned and showed in pictures, then let's take a look at what overlapping bear tracks look like.

I took this picture in the Bluff Creek area of Northern California where thousands of Bigfoot tracks were documented throughout the 1960's, it in no way resembles any of the tracks found there, or anywhere for that matter.

In the following photograph there are actually three black bear impressions, I cast this impression, which was the only example of this in the entire line of bear tracks I found.

The picture of the two casts following the picture of the impression shows this overlapping set of bear tracks alongside a 17 inch Sasquatch footprint found in the same area in the 1960's, demonstrating a clear difference.

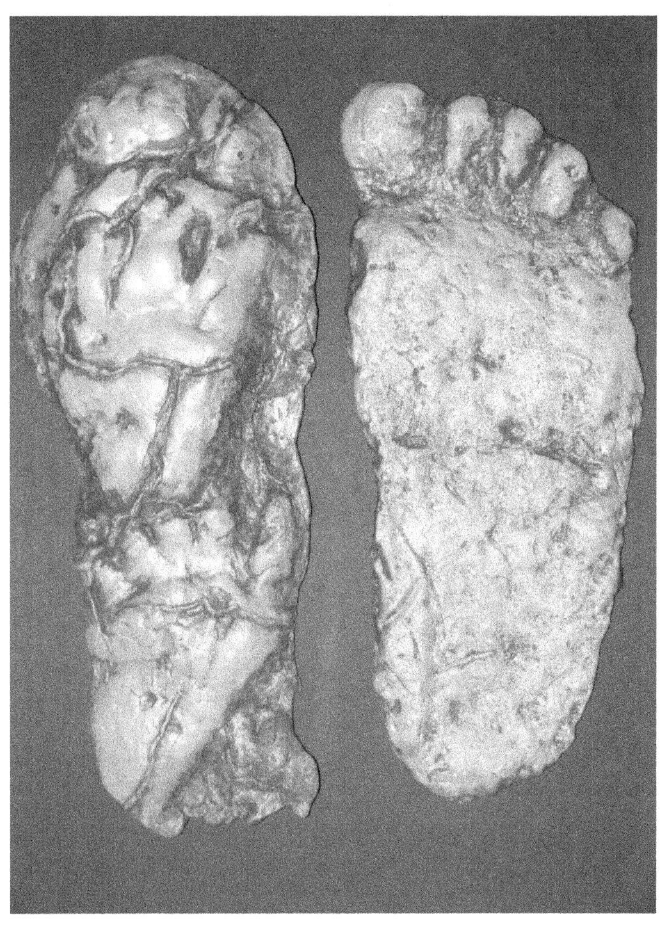

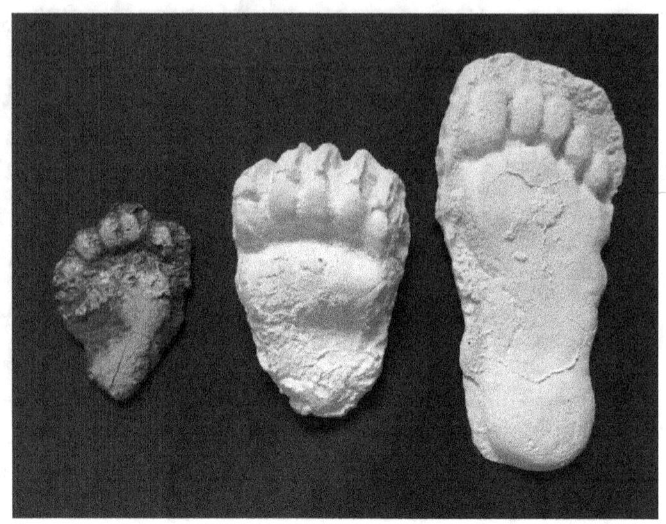

(From left to right: Black bear, Brown bear and 16 inch Sasquatch)

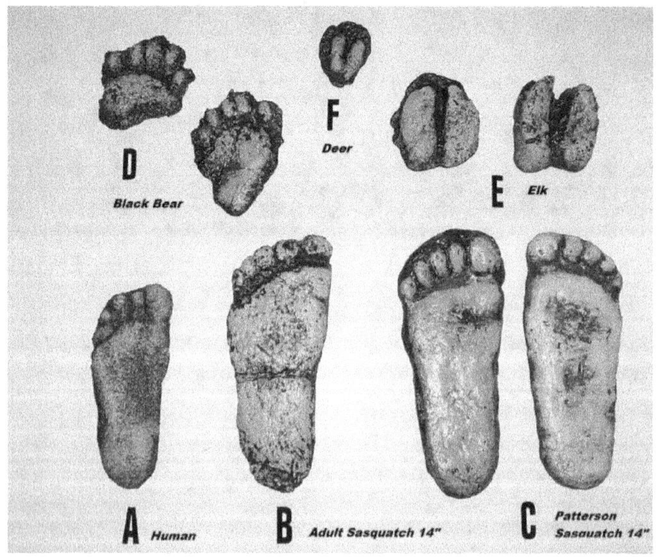

It would be very difficult to confuse one for another.

I mentioned some of the characteristics Bigfoot have that are more similar to large primates such as Gorillas or Chimps, but a couple features they have are more similar to humans. Their feet, aside from size which range in adults from 13 inches to 18 inches in overall length in adults, have a more general appearance more similar to humans. The following pictures show this.

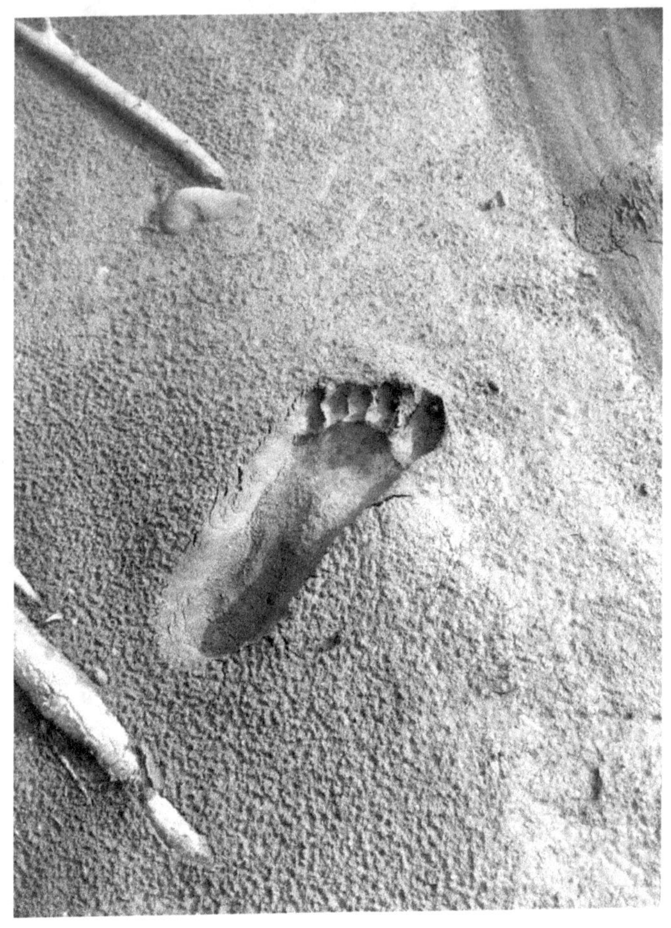

Typically Bigfoot is reported as walking on two legs very similar to human walking, however they also are able to move on all fours similar to Gorillas and Chimpanzees.

This is likely an intermediate stage in development, and bipedal locomotion is not unique to humans, as science learns more about primate evolution they have discovered that humans are only the latest primate to develop bipedal walking, it has existed in other species millions of years before us.

In forests it would be very easy to mistake a Sasquatch as a bear if it were moving on all fours, and I have had people in official positions that have witnessed this, thinking at first what they were seeing was simply a bear until it stood up and walked away on two legs.

The previous sketch shows the Bigfoot moving on all fours, note the position of the hands, walking on knuckles is common among other primate species that use thus form of locomotion. The following photograph is an example of Sasquatch knuckles in soil.

The following pictures show a comparison of human cast next to a Bigfoot hand cast, and some impressions of hand markings on automobile glass.

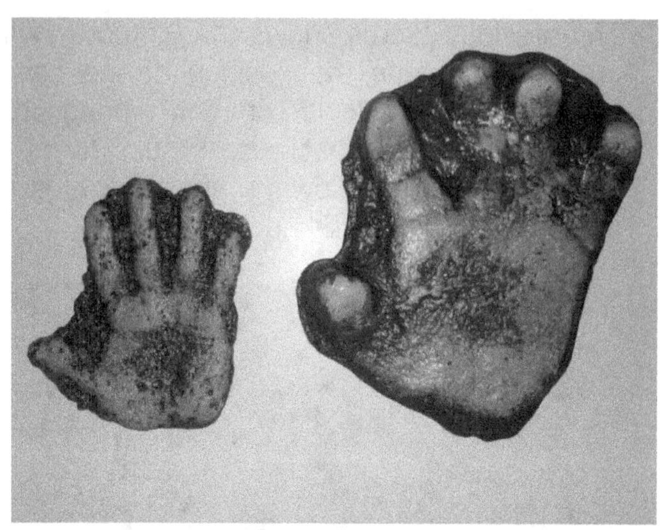

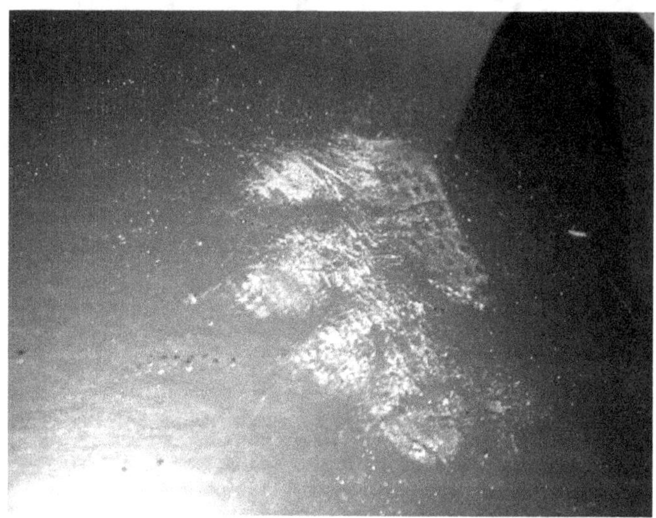

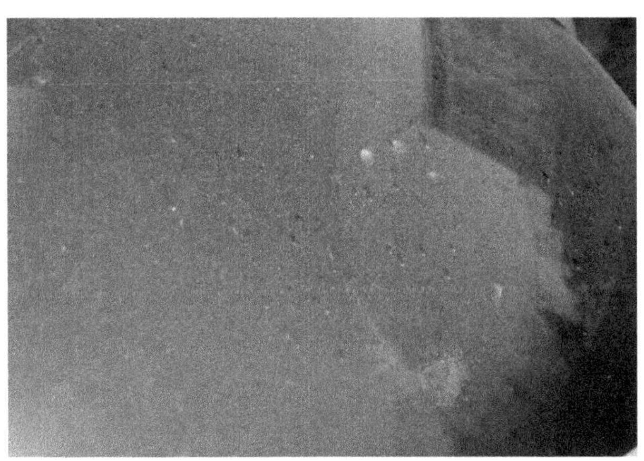

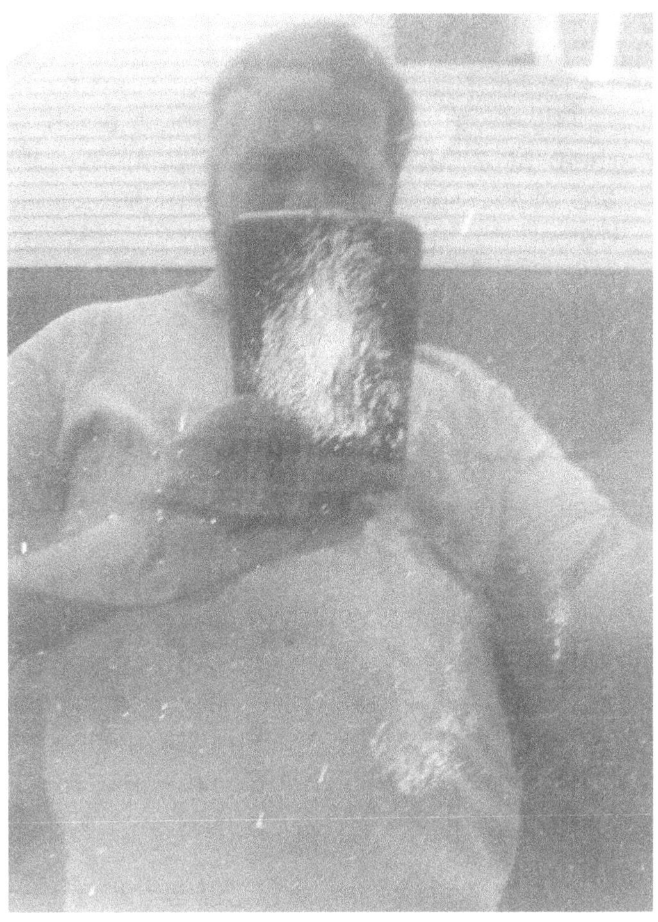

It seems Bigfoot has an interest in touching automobile glass at times. Other features are that they are covered in hair, and there are 22 variations depending on what region they are in. Hair covering and length can vary as doe's appearance.

3: behaviors

Any discussion of Bigfoot must begin with them as a social creature. All primate species are highly social creatures, and Bigfoot is no exception. In the early days of investigators looking into Bigfoot, it was believed, and many today still believe, that the Sasquatch is a solitary creature.

Thus is not correct, many encounters with the creatures, witnesses report seeing more than one individual or hear vocals and other noises indicating the presence of more than one creature.

Just because someone only sees one Bigfoot does not mean there are others of its group are not nearby. Being a primate there should always be others of the creature seen in relative close proximity.

One famous example of this is the Patterson film of 1967. In August of that year loggers discovered three sets of Bigfoot footprints on a logging road that ultimately got Roger Patterson and his friend Bob Gimlin to travel from Yakima Washington to Bluff Creek California in October of the same year. After spending three weeks searching the area, they came upon a solitary Bigfoot and Patterson captured it on film.

I personally asked Bob Gimlin in the early 1990's why he and Patterson did not follow the creature Patterson filmed. Gimlin's response was "we did not know the other two Sasquatch's location and were afraid to follow it".

Like any species, there are many behaviors, but I will provide a general listing here.

Vocals are something often reported; I personally have heard many such vocals over the past five decades. Depending on how far away the creatures are from one, loudness is a notable feature and obviously produced from a large set of lungs.

Native American tribes have said they mimic the sounds of known animals such as owls and ravens. Whistling is the most notable sound Native peoples have attributed to the Sasquatch as commonly featured in Native ceremonial masks, the whistling lips are prominent.

Curiosity is a common primate behavior; Bigfoot will often look at objects in its environment that is not naturally occurring.

One example of this is when in 1958, bulldozer operator Jerry Crew found large manlike footprints circling his machine one morning. Newspaper writer for the Eureka Times, Andrew Genzoli went to look at the footprints with Jerry Crew. Crew made an offhand comment that "that fellow sure has big feet" and Genzoli coined the term Bigfoot. But in the bluff creek region from 1958 to 1967 the creatures often appeared during the night to look at and also manipulate manmade objects, even picking up 55 gallon drums of fuel and throwing a road grader tire into a gully.

Most often this curiosity is food related, and they will venture near human farms or homes for livestock or pet foods. Most often like other primate species, in their environment they will avoid objects that do not belong, especially manmade objects.

The Sasquatch is most often seen at night, but is seen during the day time as well, so they are not true nocturnal creatures. The time frame they are most active is around dusk and again at dawn.

Wildlife and domestic animals have been reported as fearing the Sasquatch and will run or hide when the creature are present.

The Sasquatch seems to have a disagreeable temperament and angers quickly and often has a vindictive quality. At times they have killed livestock without any obvious purpose than to kill. This behavior also exists in other primate species, and is not uncommon.

The Sasquatch like other primate species will usually let you know when it or they do not want humans in their location. They often are reported to throw objects at humans. Anything from pine cones to sticks, and rocks. I interviewed a witness that saw one of the creatures and it threw its feces at him, hitting him and he said the force was such that he felt injured.

We see this very behavior commonly among chimpanzees and Gorillas.

This is a warming, and if you should happen to see the creatures or start having objects flying from the woods in your direction it is a warning to leave, and should be heeded!

Witnesses at times report the creatures baring their teeth at the witness, in anthropology this is another common primate behavior called a "lip flip". In nature actual combat can become a death sentence if one or more participants of an encounter actually engage in a fight. Even scratches can become infected and the individual could die so combat is most often avoided. One way to demonstrate ones superiority in an encounter is to show off potential weapons. In primates its teeth and this display usually works. It is another warning to go away as with the throwing of objects and should be taken very seriously.

At times the creatures will run alongside a moving car or truck, the reason is unknown.

Slapping the sides of buildings, this is done to determine how many humans are present.

Making sounds people call "wood knocking", wood against wood in the forest is not a good way to communicate, and this sound, no matter the force will not carry very far. In actuality the sounds reported by witnesses is tongue popping. This is also done by other primate species, and sounds similar to the name given to this sound; however it is unknown why it is done.

Glowing eyes; when light is shined on the creatures at night often they reflect light similar to other animals. Sometimes it has been reported as having a red tinge, but often it is amber in color or a light bluish. The light source is most often the reason for the differences in color. The Sasquatch eye does not have any bioluminescence, no mammal has this.

Trail cameras do not work in getting photographic images of Bigfoot for two primary reasons. 1: manmade objects in their environment are a huge red flag, all primates are some of the most intelligent creatures on the planet, and they are intimately aware of what does and does not belong where they live. They will avoid these making wide movements around them. 2: game cameras use infrared light to focus; the Sasquatch can see infrared light so again they will avoid these objects.

4: Diet

Skeptics once proclaimed Bigfoot could not have enough food to survive, therefore could not be real. This was a false assumption. The Sasquatch is an apex predator, there are many examples of witnesses seeing them kill and eat animals. Bigfoot is a large primate, and accordingly will have a large brain. Having a large brain requires a lot or protein to power it. That means eating meat.

The Sasquatch is an ambush predator, meaning they will conserve energy while waiting for a meal to come along then in a quick burst of energy catch prey.

They are the top predator in their environment. Even large brown bears have been witnessed fleeing from a Bigfoot once the bear became aware of the creatures presence.

The Sasquatch is also an opportunist; they will sneak in near human's dwellings and campsites and take food items, similar to what bears do.

The Sasquatch is very skilled at hunting; they are extremely stealthy and can remain motionless for long time periods. Witnesses at times at first think they see a creature, but then decide its nothing more than a stump and their minds playing tricks on them until they later go to the place they at first thought they saw something to learn what they saw was gone.

Chimpanzees do this often, standing perfectly still for long time periods in the wild, and humans have walked past them unaware the chimp was present.

Bigfoot has been witnessed doing the same thing.

So what does a Sasquatch eat? The following is a partial list, but gives a good demonstration that they have abundant food available to them.

the Sasquatch on average needs a minimum of approximately 15,000 calories daily to survive. Large silverbacks Gorillas need approximately 8,000 calories a day, and a friend of mine in Scotland recently told me that a friend of his who is 6'9" and is current title holder of strongest man, can consume upwards of 14,000 calories a day in training.

These silverback gorillas on average weight around 485 pounds, and the Sasquatch seems to be much larger so the figure of 15,000 calories a day seems reasonable given their size.

Grizzly bears can consume up to 58,000 calories in a day, and they as a species they do quite well in North America.

If the Sasquatch needs at least 15,000 calories a day to survive, what is available in North America for them to eat? The following is only a partial list, but the reader will see that there are numerous sources of sustenance available for a large omnivore to not only survive, but thrive upon in North America. The following is a partial list, remember most animals meat is approximately 700 calories per pound. Before we look at the list, let us consider a deer as an example, these calculations are approximations only for our discussion, and will be different in specific situations.

A deer weigh approximately 150 pounds; their meat has a value of 712 calories per pound. If we multiply the total weight of the deer by the caloric value, we get a figure of 106,800 calories. If we divide the caloric needs of the Sasquatch which is an average of 15,000 calories each day we get 7.12 which is the number of Sasquatch's one deer could sustain each day. It is no coincidence groups of Sasquatch's number approximately 4 to 6 individuals. This calculation suggests that each group of Sasquatch could be sustained by a single deer each day, but they are constantly in search of food, and supplement their diet with more than deer. The following is the partial list I mentioned previously, and will show they do indeed have plenty to sustain them and thrive in the environments of North America.

North American mammals:

Elk, Bear (brown and black), seals, walrus,

manatee, mountain goat, Dalls sheep, Barbary sheep, bighorn sheep, American bison, muskox, fallow deer, white tailed deer, mule deer, caribou, moose, feral horse, mountain lion, jaguar, ocelot, lynx, bob cat, wolves, coyote, foxes, feral pig, collared peccary, sea otter, northern river otter, wolverine, badger, skunk, American marten, weasels, raccoon, opossum, armadillo, porcupine, marmot, woodchuck, beaver, nutria, muskrat, rabbits, squirrels, prairie dogs, chipmunks, pikas, voles, lemmings, rats, mice.

Of course there are a variety of fish, birds, reptiles such as alligators and many varieties of plants, berries mushrooms, etc. The list would be a very long one if we knew all that the Sasquatch eat, we must also consider domestic livestock, pets, and the foods we have for domestic animals and even our own trash.

5: Markings and Sign

Sasquatch territorial markings are most often ignored as nothing more than weather damage.

Usually they will snap over a healthy young tree as shown in the following example:

The above tree was one that I discovered in July 1991 in Southwest Washington State. This was freshly broken over; it was inside a closed canopy of mature trees. The break measured 8 feet one inch above the ground. The tree was healthy. I subsequently found twelve more of these same trees that all measured approximately three inches thick at the break and in a line going to the north east, and approximately one hundred yards apart. No other vegetation or trees were damaged in any way in this area.

I showed pictures of the trees I found to a Native American friend from the Klamath Reservation in Southern Oregon, and he told me this was a Sasquatch marking, and the line of trees broken at this location was sign for the rest of the group feeding there to move to the next feeding area, indicating the direction by the line of breaks.

Snapping a tree over at a 90 degree angle is just one kind of marking, twisting a tree is another, and the following are a few examples. Again these were done in warm, summer conditions, no wind or animal sign. These trees were twisted, as one might wring water from a cloth.

The significance or meaning is not known, or why they might snap over one tree and twist another.

One might think this is a common sight in the forested regions of North America, and this question came up during a recent field excursion my team and I took in Southern Oregon. I said for the team to watch carefully as we drove 30 miles from one location through the forest to another location, and to count these markings as we traversed the forest. When we reached our destination, they had seen no markings of this type.

If this tree breaking or twisting were common and the result of weather, or disease then it should be a common sight. However this is not normally the case.

The weight of snow in the winter will do this, however the height of the breaks will be much higher than the average six to eight feet of Bigfoot markings.

For there to be such a large creature in the forests, it should leave other sign of its presence. Like other wildlife, their scat should be present, and it is.

In the early 1960's a couple of the first people to begin looking into the possibility of Bigfoot's existence would find huge piles of scat in the now famous Bluff Creek area of Northern California and the place where Roger Patterson and Bob Gimlin shot a film of a Sasquatch in 1967.

Bob Titmus and logging contractor Ray Wallace conducted some volumetric tests on some of the unusual scat they had been finding. The result was that this scat was equal to that excreted from a 1200 pound horse. Bears do not excrete this volume, not even brown bears.

First let's look at bear scat:

Black Bear:

Shape is tubular similar to humans, it size is around two inches thick and five to twelve inches long.

Contents; it's usually filled with vegetation and insects. When berries are available it is globular filled with berries and seeds. Bears are omnivores so small animals or deer and moose remains may be in the scat.

Color; it can range from black to brown, when a bear is eating a mixed diet, and green when eating mostly grasses.

Brown bear scat:

Shape is the same as black bear and similar in content. Size is two inches thick or more. It may appear similar to a "cow pile" when eating fruits and berries.

Coloration is the same as black bear. Brown bear is almost the same as brown bear, with the possible exception of size.

Sasquatch: scat is very different, The shape most often is similar to the appearance of human scat as with bears, but size and quantity are much greater. The following pictures are of two different Sasquatch scat; both found in different parts of Northern California.

(Sutter creek California)

(Hyampom area)

Bigfoot scat is massive, thickness is often

two inches to four plus inches thick, and be twelve inches to twenty four inches in length. Easily comparing the volume to the twelve hundred pound horse volume Bob Titmus tested.

Coloration, Bigfoot scat is typically dark colored indicating a heavy protein diet. They will supplement their diet with berries and fruits and other vegetation, and at times human garbage.

Once I dissected a Bigfoot scat to determine what it had been eating, and found a complete plastic bag like grocery stores use in the produce section, clearly showing the creature had been consuming human trash.

Often the Sasquatch has been discovered to defecate in streams or lakes. Witnesses have seen this behavior, and most likely this is to keep their presence in an area hidden from the other wildlife there.

Smaller predators will often mark ownership of a hunting area using their scat, larger predators will establish dominance by depositing their scat on top of the smaller predators scat. The Sasquatch being a primate is far superior in intelligence, and will hide its scat.

Most animals flee the area a Sasquatch group is feeding in once its discovered they are present, this is why they hide it in water.

Conversely, I have found on rare occasions they have deposited it in places driving game sources into channeled locations, resulting in choke points for ambushing prey.

But this behavior is rare.

6: What to do if you encounter a Bigfoot?

There are many opinions as to Sasquatch nature today, most are wrong. There is the "friendly forest dweller line of thought" or the "shy solitary creatures of the forest", to Name just a couple.

These are nothing more than personal fanciful anthropomorphized opinions of a few.

Historical accounts by the dozens provide the true nature of these creatures, and yes at times they can be man eaters.

I will provide two accounts from pre-1960 demonstrating the creature's behaviors.

The first was an article in Sports Afield Magazine from 1963, the events of the story were likely twenty years earlier.

''The story is titled "Long Hunter – Alaskan Style" by Russell Annabel. The story is about a mountain man named Tex Cobb, who spent years trapping in Canada and Alaska

The Denna people liked him, Tex Cobb. No sentiment was wasted on either side, but he and the tribesmen had a live and let live understanding that was rare in those days. He stayed off their trap lines, and they stayed off his. If an Indian had a salmon net in an eddy, Tex found another eddy, and vice versa. Due to the fact that the Indians trusted him, we became involved with what today would be called, I suppose an abominable snowman. I have since heard and read a great deal about the abominable snowman. I have seen the photographs of those tracks in the snow on a Tibetan mountain, and to me they are simply the tracks of a man with gunnysack or some cloth wrapped around his feet as protection from the cold, climbing slew foot because the slope was steep and he had no crampons. But when I was a youngster roaming the North with Tex, we had never heard of the abominable snowman. We had, however, heard much about Gilyuk; the shaggy cannibal giant sometimes called the big man with the little hat.

Our adventure with Gilyuk occurred while we were camped in a pretty spruce park on Yellow jacket Creek, south of Tyrone Lake. We had spent the entire summer on this mountain – girt Nelchina Plateau, wandering about in aimless nomad fashion. Tex said we were prospecting and looking for fur sign. Maybe we were. He always had to have an excuse for enjoying the country, a commercial excuse if he could think of one. Anyway, it was now late September, the beautiful time, no mosquitoes, the land ablaze with color, the fish and the meat animal's summer fat, the caribou horde gathering, and we were footloose and free as perhaps men can never be again. This morning Tex was making coffee, and I was down at the creek cleaning a mess of grayling for breakfast, when six Indians filed through the timber. They stood for a moment solemnly regarding our four horses. To them a horse was a rarity, a mysterious animal. They called them

McKinley moose, because McKinley was the only president they had ever heard of, and the horses were as big as moose. I followed them to the camp.

"Have you eaten?" Tex asked them in Denna.

They said they had eaten. Chief Stickman was with them. I had seen him once before, at Eklutna Village. A squat, square – faced man, very dark, with long hair and quick – moving obsidian eyes, he was the Denna boss of this entire area, and his reputation was bad. But now he had trouble that he couldn't handle. He told us about it, and as he talked, he kept standing first on one leg, then the other, balancing himself with the moccasined sole of the free foot against the knee of the supporting leg. I don't know whether it was habit or a medicine trick to ward off evil spirits, or both, but it was disconcerting. He had come into this area two days ago, he said, with some of his people to kill and cache caribou for winter use. But they had discovered that

Gilyuk, the shaggy giant, was hanging around. They found his sign yesterday. And of course everybody knew that Gilyuk wasn't interested in caribou. Gilyuk ate men.

"What kind of sign" Tex asked.

"We will take you to see it," Stickman said. "It's not far."

After breakfast we followed the Indians upstream a couple of miles to a burned flat on which a nurse crop of aspen and birch had grown. In the center of the flat stood a ruined birch sapling. It had been about four inches through and maybe ten feet tall. Something had twisted the sapling as a man would twist a matchstick. The wood had separated into individual fibers; the bark hung in tatters. Stickman and his hunters stood back, while Tex and I looked the site over. Moose often ride a sapling down to get at the tender upper twigs. So do caribou. But no moose or caribou had done this. This had been done by something with hands. It had happened yesterday, because the leaves of the sapling had not yet completely wilted. It wasn't the work of lightening – no burns. A freak whirlwind hadn't done it, because trees and brush a few yards distant were undamaged. The hard ground showed no tracks. We found no snagged hair on the brush. Absolutely nothing except the incredibly twisted birch sapling. It was without question the eeriest sight I have ever beheld in the wilds.

Stickman said, "It is Gilyuk's mark. We have seen it before."

I wish to make clear that to the Denna people Gilyuk was no legendary creature their grandfathers had told them about. He was a reality, and they spoke of him as they spoke of bears and wolves. They saw his sign, and they saw him. He was a shaggy giant who wore a little hat and ate men. "We want to ask you to camp with us until we have killed our caribou," Stickman said. "Gilyuk doesn't molest white men. Perhaps he will not molest us if you are in the camp."   Stickman had already told us that he was bivouacked on the shore of a pothole lake two hours to the eastward.

Tex said all right, we would move to his camp in the morning. As he was still looking at the twisted sapling, his green eyes narrowed in thought. I couldn't take my gaze off it either.

Stickman said, "Thanks, Kosaki," a strange word of respect, held over from the Old Russian Cossack, and we parted company with the Indians.

Next morning I brought the horses in at daybreak. We ate, broke camp and were putting on the packs, when here came the Indians, all of them – all, that is except Stickman. An old man told us Stickman was dead, he said. Gilyuk had taken him. The chief had got up in the night and gone down to the lake, perhaps for water, but nobody knew. A squaw with a birch – bark torch found his red flannel underwear on the gravel beach. It had been torn off him. There may have been tracks, but the entire hunting party had swarmed over the beach, and by daylight no tracker on earth could have made sense of the jumble.

Well, until the day of his own death last July, while on a sentimental journey to a fateful spot in Cook Inlet, Tex was convinced that the cannibal giant Gilyuk killed Stickman. When asked if he believed in the existence of abominable snowmen, Tex would reply that he didn't think there were any around in Alaska nowadays, but that they had existed, at least one of them, a couple of decades back".

The second account is from Southern Oregon 1890 titled the Chetco Monster.

"The logging operation was a small one, employing a dozen men whose families lived in tents alongside the river. For several weeks nothing unusual happened. Occasionally garbage cans were overturned at night by marauding bears. Sometimes the beasts were so troublesome that an armed guard stood by while loggers felled the big trees. At the campsite mothers watched their young children closely and forbade older boys and girls to play hide-and-seek in the forest.

Even when they swam in the shallow river, an adult kept a sharp lookout for bears.

Then one morning enormously large human footprints were discovered along the riverbanks. The loggers laughingly accused one another of having feet as big as chopping blocks. Everyone, from oldest to youngest in camp, measured his footprints against those of the unknown visitor. Since no one's feet were that large, one question was bandied about repeatedly: If those weren't a bear's tracks, whose were they?

Someone said there was a "Wildman" living way up the river. He was an irritable old devil who threatened to shoot anyone who approached his cabin. No matter how bad the weather was he never wore a hat or boots. He was always bareheaded and barefooted.

Barefooted? Then the tracks were his? With the mystery of the tracks happily solved, the people promptly forgot them. But several nights later the sound of eerie whistling and angry shrieks wakened them.

In every tent men bounded out of bed and grabbed their guns, assuming there was a wounded bear nearby. No one lighted a lamp for fear of attracting the beast, and frightened children were warned not to cry.

The spine chilling noises went on and on. Sometimes they seemed close by, other times from the direction of the road or the river. But finally the sounds faded into the distance, and quiet returned to the dark campsite. At daybreak the men gathered to talk. They debated whether it was a bear or mountain lion.

To satisfy themselves and ease their families worries, a half dozen men searched about for bear or mountain lion tracks, however, at the edge of the clearing beyond the first stand of trees and dense undergrowth they came upon more of the giant sized human footprints. The men debated whether it was the old recluse.

They agreed they had to catch the demented man before he killed someone. So, as quiet;ly as possible the search party backtracked along the line of footprints. These led them out onto the road several hundred yards above the camp and up the road to the logging site. Here they found where the Wildman had emerged from the forest into the open area and had prowled around tree stumps, piles of bushes and the machinery used loading the logs onto wagons.

Then the men had a nasty shock. Massive unwieldy tree limbs, far too heavy for one man to handle, had been pulled out of the tangled waste piles and either tossed aside like match sticks or used to beat on the machinery.

The searchers followed the tracks back down the road into the forest. For the first time they noticed shrubs torn to pieces and saplings uprooted and whacked to shreds.

This explained the thudding and snapping sounds heard during the night. The footprints circled the camp, went down the well-beaten path to the river turning back to the road, went down it a half mile and turned off into the forest.

The men pressed on as far as they dared. However, when the tracks plunged down into a steep ravine, they stopped. The gloomy depths provided too many hiding places for a demented killer.

The Chetco Indians believed there were man-animals in the woods, the logger informed his friends. He had heard the story from a white man whom the Indians trusted enough to take him into their confidence. They claimed that for generations they had shared their hunting grounds with fierce-looking hairy creatures that walked upright like men.

The strange beings were not human, nor animal. Neither friendly nor hostile. They were simply there, like every other man or wild creature, so the Indians left them alone.

But very late on the third night the frightening sounds were once again heard faintly from far off in the woods. People jerked upright in bed. As the whistling and screaming grew louder, in every tent men pulled on their trousers and boots, and readied their guns. Obviously the night prowler was coming closer and closer. When he seemed only fifty feet away, one man took desperate action. Hastily fashioning a torch of oily rags and kindling, he set fire to it. Torch in one hand and rifle in the other, he raced into the woods.

Meanwhile the man's wife called for help. Within minutes several men stumbled toward her in the darkness. They groaned when they learned that their comrade had gone into the woods alone. None hesitated to follow, but minutes passed while one dashed off to fetch a lantern and others supplied themselves with extra cartridges.

Finally the party headed into the forest in the direction from which the awful sounds were heard. They had covered only a short distance when the whistling and shrieking stopped.

The men halted, and listened. There was a long silence, then an outburst of bestial yowling followed by human screams. Thinking their friend was being attacked; the men fought through the undergrowth, the man with the lantern in the lead. Moments later their comrade appeared and collapsed in their arms. At first he was too terrified to speak.

His companions fired their guns to drive off the howler and then waited patiently for the poor man to gasp out the details. He said that by torchlight he had followed the line of giant sized footprints and suddenly came upon a huge creature covered with hair.

"A bear? No, an ape! A monstrous ape, seven or eight feet tall, two axe handles wide (shoulders or approximate) with beady yellow eyes and bared teeth.

The torchlight must have blinded it because it stood stock still, one hand shading its eyes.

Then it let out a tremendous roar.

The man hurled his torch into its face, but instead of shooting it, the frightened man ran screaming toward camp.

While his companions did not doubt his word, they asked anxiously if he was sure the beast was an ape. "Yes he was positive". It really looked like an ape? Yes, an ape. Did it have fangs? You bet! Claws? The man said sarcastically that he hadn't stayed around long enough to study the brute. But after thinking it over, he said it had hands like a man, only twice as large and covered with hair right down to the fingernails.

After that they all decided to return to camp. After much discussion the loggers agreed to take turns standing guard day and night until the ape was captured or shot.

Two men would patrol the campsite on two hour watches while the rest worked or slept. Since women present knew how to handle a gun, their assistance during daylight hours was welcomed. The older boys and girls offered to gather firewood so that large fires could be kept blazing all night.

Nothing unusual happened during the day or the early night hours, but the two whose turn came about two am asked the men they were to relieve to stand by.

They wanted to slip into the woods and really search for the ape. Reluctantly the one patrol agreed to stand by while their relief party set out on their ape hunt.

The hunters carried a small lantern because without some light they could not follow any tracks. But they were careful to keep the light at ground level. Their rifles were loaded, and the safety catches thumbed back. Not long after, they came upon bits of charred cloth amidst a welter of huge footprints. This must be where their friend had thrown his torch at the monster.

Yes, there were his boot marks. Examining the area closely they found where the ape had turned deeper into the forest, Instead of backtracking to the road. They followed gingerly step by step over and around ferns, shrubs, outcroppings and rocks and massive tree trunks.

What happened next could only be guessed. Apparently the apelike creature loomed before them. One man started shooting while the other put down the lantern and shot too. The patrol on guard at the campsite heard the volley of shots. They pounded each other happily.

The hunters had killed the beast! But then they listened in mounting horror to frantic cries for help, which were drowned out by horrendous shrieks and roaring.

The awful noises continued for some moments and then faded out. The silence was even more frightening to the guards.

They shouted for help and soon were surrounded by armed loggers and their wives. After a hasty explanation, all the men plunged into the woods, leaving the women to build up the fires and protect the children.

The searchers shouted, swung lanterns and fired their guns so that their friends would know help was on the way.

After advancing some distance they stopped briefly and called to the men. When neither responded, they fired shots. No answering shots were heard. Once more the party advanced. Before long they came upon a gruesome sight. Their friends were dead.

Judging from bloodstains, their bodies had been slammed against tree trunks and torn to pieces. A trail of blood smeared footprints led off into the forest. The beast obviously had been wounded but no man present was willing to track it through the dark forest. Some did volunteer to gather up the remains of their unfortunate comrades while others returned to camp for blankets, and break the sad news.

Within twenty four hours the campsite was deserted. The logging operation moved to another location.

A professional hunter with trained dogs was hired to assist hunters in tracking down the savage beast. It was never captured nor its voice ever heard again. The most people could hope for was that it had crawled into a well hidden lair, and died.

These are frightening accounts, and should be taken as cautionary events. Even if you do not believe such creatures exist, why take any unnecessary chances in the wild?

There are many reasons for caution while out hiking or other forest activities.

Since the 1970's human behaviors toward wildlife and the forests has changed greatly. Throughout our history Humans have humans had a very violent behavior towards wildlife, we after all are apex predators ourselves, and wildlife gave us a wide birth

Since the 1970's we have stopped indiscriminately stopped shooting at all animals in the wild. This has also caused changes in the behavior of wildlife, we hear more and more reports of mountain lions stalking and sometimes attacking hikers.

Sometimes cougars do kill people, and coyotes are more often approaching homes and pets and even children are at risk.

So if we believe a large primate species inhabits the forests or not, we should still use caution.

Here are some safety tips to use when in the forests:

1: Never go alone, this is probably the top behavior that could result in problems up to even death. Many of us don't think twice about going for a hike on a sunny day to enjoy nature, but even a simple stumble over a rock or root can result in severe injury, and if no one comes along to help, one could end up with hypothermia and die. So it is best to go with another person.

Bigfoot is an opportunist; a lone person may or may not interest one, but if there is one that is disposed to attacking a human for an easy meal, the n two or more people is a deterrent.

The Sasquatch does not always attack and eat humans, but some do so there is no need to chance this, I have numerous examples. One such incident was told to be by a woman in Missouri, she told me that a neighbor of hers told her that one day she was alone near her garden when she was hit on the side of her head, rendering her unconscious.

She awoke moments later and observed this enormous creature standing over her, and then she blacked out again. When she awoke once more, this creature had opened her stomach and was in the process of eating her small intestine; fortunately for this woman another neighbor came to her aid, chasing the creature away.

With the many people that simply vanish in the forests, it is wise to leave nothing to chance, and to return home safely.

The Sasquatch have many of the same or similar behaviors other primate species exhibit. One is mock charging. I have interviewed numerous people that were in this situation.

Primates are all territorial, and at times will charge a person or animal invading their territory. This normally is not an actual attack, but rather a strong warning to leave immediately.

Typically the sight of such a creature causes a person to temporarily go into shock, and they stand still and the creature leaves. As with Gorillas that mock charge, standing still is also the best course of action until the tension has lowered and the person on the receiving end of the charge can leave.

Other behaviors that tell you to leave immediately are as previously mentioned such as the "lip flip" or the Sasquatch showing you its teeth, or the creatures throwing objects at you. These are all strong messages to leave the area, and I do recommend this course of action!

What do Native peoples say about what to do when encountering a Bigfoot? Here is one:

This comes from an interview I did with a man that took part in a native American talk.

"Chief walks over and stands right in front of him and says do you think there's humor in this? And he goes, there's no such thing. And he goes really? So he starts a slideshow presentation. And he started showing about people that had been found out that had been killed by these things. And he actually had a rifle there that he pulled out that isn't just twisted. There's no way you were I could have done this, this thing or this thing. It just wouldn't happen. And he told about what to do if you ran in into these things. And he says this is very critical on how to not get hurt. He says these things consider your hands a weapon. He said if you encounter one of these things; do not look at in the eye. He said you sort of tilt your head down to keep an eye on it and you turn your palms out. If you have your weapon on you, You swing it over your back. You turn your palms out and you just back away. You don't show any aggression whatsoever. Back out of there and just start walking. And once you get back where you feel comfortable, you turn to the side we keep walking but you keep your palms where they can see them. Then you can turn your back and walk and he said anybody's ever done that is never been attacked".

Very sound advice, and I have heard this from other Native sources.

If you should happen to encounter a Sasquatch, do not look it directly in the eye, In the primate world this is a sign of aggression so avoid it!

Leave the area the way you came, do not run or panic as this could trigger a predatory response. Simply walk back the way you came.

If you encounter a Sasquatch that has a strong odor, this is a sign of it being surprised and/or agitated. If the creature is moving or swaying from side to side, this is also a sign of agitation, you want to leave quickly.

If you encounter a Sasquatch that appears to be jumping up and down in a stationary spot, this is also a sign of agitation.

If you happen to be alone and encounter one or more Bigfoot, talking out loud as if calling to or speaking to other people nearby will stop any aggression by the creatures. It is a numbers thing with them, if they think you are alone, this could lead them to aggressive behaviors, but numbers of humans cause them to be more wary. Humans are pack hunters, and while not nearly as robust as the Sasquatch, are formidable in numbers, and they would know this having been around humans for thousands of years.

This method has been very successful.

If you are armed with a gun, **DO NOT SHOOT AT A SASQUATCH!** This is an act of aggression to them, and they will likely attack you, again leave the area. My only advice other than leaving is if you are being attacked, and you have no other choice but to shoot. Remember, the Sasquatch is never alone, they live in groups typically of 4 to 6 individuals, maybe more and the group members are nearby. If you attempt to harm one, the others will attack.

If you see one near a road you are driving on, do not stop to look at it, they have been known to rip car doors off the vehicle and take occupants out. This is not a safari; your vehicle is no guarantee of safety.

Pets will often alert you to their presence; they will run or attempt to hide.

If they are encroaching on your home, they will often ramp up behaviors such as testing the limits of your motion sensors; they will watch for patterns in your behaviors and use them to their advantage in moving in closer.

They want cover or concealment when

approaching human dwellings, cut any brush or trees back at least 50 feet from around your dwelling, this will help stop the encroachment.

In the animal world, the strongest smell if often belonging to the top predator. Pouring bleach around the boundaries of your property is a deterrent, the Sasquatch has a very strong odor and will mark places using its urine, and bleach is stronger and will assert your dominance around your property.

To the average reader, these may seem like odd advisements, but if you have experiences these creatures behaviors then they are not to unusual.

My hopes are that everyone stays safe, so I have provided some knowledge and advice. These methods have been given to people that have asked me for help, and they have worked in each case.

Enjoy nature and be safe above all else, if I

can be of assistance to anyone, I can be
reached at wjevning@gmail.com

95

ABOUT THE AUTHOR

William Jevning is a two time witness of direct Sasquatch encounters, has spent the past five decades conducting field investigations and research into the subject of the Sasquatch. Previous books are Notes From the Field, In Search of the Unknown, Haunted valley, The Minnesota Iceman, Witness of the Unknown volumes 1 and 2 and Bigfoot Field Work 101 and Bigfoot Evidence. He has been on television shows such Americas Book of Secrets, The Mystery of Bigfoot and radio and podcasts, is the hoist of the current podcast Creek Devil. He can be reached at wjevning@gmail.com

www.ingramcontent.com/pod-product-compliance
Lightning Source LLC
Chambersburg PA
CBHW061245250726

48653CB00002B/515